Nightmares, Nonsense
and
Nursery Rhymes

The complete lyrics of Shadowland with
insights and anecdotes

by

Clive Nolan

CONTENTS

Introduction

Now, let me think… The band Shadowland emerged from a long succession of other projects and bands that I had been a part of. A quick ramble through some of my history might help to give some context.

Band and Beginnings

From my later school days came a group called Sleepwalker which lasted into my time at University (in different guises). This was a five-piece progressive rock band, and my first band. I think of this as very much a learning ground for what I was to do in later years. Ironically, one of the biggest gigs we ever did was while we were all still at school. That school, by the way, was King's School, Gloucester. Our debut gig was held in the school hall. I have little doubt that we were fairly awful, but since that hall had not seen many rock concerts, it was full to capacity. You could say it was downhill from there.

Anyway, this is not a book about Sleepwalker, although that might make an interesting retrospective! As a band we stumbled along for about five years, taking me from school through to university, although the line-up changed a lot over the years. We did do quite a few gigs, which certainly provided a great training ground, and most of the time, we wondered what on earth we were doing these gigs for! We were losing money and morale in our search for 'rock stardom'!

Sounds and Skateboards

Over time I became bored with the 'rock band' format and changed things for a more electronic outfit called Danzante. Now, this did not have a progressive rock bone in its body! It was a three-piece instrumental band – two keyboard players and a percussionist (mainly Latin percussion). The keyboard players also utilised sequencers and drum machines… pretty cutting edge back in the mid-eighties!

Around this time, I remember going to the Marquee Club in Wardour Street, London to see Marillion (this is before they were even signed). Howard Jones was supporting. In case you do not know this artist, he is a singer songwriter who originally went out on his own with a bank of keyboards and sequencers as his 'band'.

This was a brave move when supporting a progressive rock band, where the audience was far from 'progressive' in attitude. He was heckled a lot and eventually someone threw something, and he left the stage. A minute later, Fish came on stage and berated the bad attitude of these few idiots in the audience, and Mr Jones returned to a big cheer. Personally, I really enjoyed his set, and loved the technology he was embracing… to me, the potential for what could be done was amazing! I think he got the last laugh from that gig at the Marquee, because not long after he was enjoying some hit singles, and a lot of fame!

I suppose Danzante was the closest I ever came to Jazz, and although we did not do many gigs, it was fun, and a valuable learning process. In those days we used to load the sequencers from information on a cassette tape! We were all music students at London University, and I think this felt like we were pioneers on this path linking music with technology.

We did play for 'Live Aid' on the day as well.

OK… it was not actually part of the 'Live Aid' concert at Wembley. It was, however, on the same day. I believe we were part of some kind of skateboard event!

And then I discovered Kate Bush!

Keyboards and Kate

Well, in truth, I re-discovered her. I always liked her stuff, but the album 'Hounds of Love' was a moment of epiphany for me. I really loved that album… still do! Great atmosphere, great melodies… and just brilliant songwriting. I always hoped that one day I would get to meet this lady, but (so far) that has never happened. I would love to tell her what an influence she had on me…. Anyway, I digress…

The 'Kate Bush' factor led me back towards songwriting (as opposed to writing instrumental pieces). Danzante became The Cast which was again a three piece – keyboards, guitar and vocals.

Anyone who has heard any of The Cast demos will surely recognise where I was headed in my songwriting style! My attempts to re-write 'Hounds of Love' or 'Cloudbusting' were rather obvious, I think. This was also the first time I worked with a female vocalist (we had two of them over the years). When the second singer left, we decided upon a male singer, and gradually The Cast was shifting back towards rock music.

Concerts and Cassettes

For a while, The Cast had what we call in the trade a 'production deal' – sort of a management deal with recording benefits. I suppose this was the first time anyone had taken what we do (and therefore what I do) seriously, so I am grateful to the Soundmill guys for giving us this opportunity. During this time, something very important happened. Despite our vague attempts to go down the Aha route, I'm not sure any of us in the band were particularly convinced by this direction. Now remember, we were a three piece, keyboards (with the use of sequencers and drum machines), guitar and singer. I used to sport one of those 'keytars' so I could be a bit more active on stage, and we had a guy off stage whose job was to re-load the various sequencers or drum machines. Naturally, that did not come without risks. I used to spend most of each song hoping that the information on the cassette was not corrupted, or we would be in trouble for the next song. I remember one time… it was the first time The Cast supported Pendragon at the Marquee… the drum machine tempo was accidentally set wrongly by the off stage guy (no I am not naming names, Derek, and after the string intro, we realised that everything was running twice the speed it should… so, I had to stop the machine, re-set and start again. Not a great feeling in front of 400 people at the Marquee. All I could think of was 'move quickly, or they will do a Howard Jones on you!' Fortunately, they were a good-natured bunch and we got through it in one piece. Someone did should out 'get a drummer', but that thought was beginning to appeal to me too.

In fact, The Cast supported Pendragon again – twice, over a three-day set of gigs at the Marquee, which we had called 'The Red Shoes Shows'. By then, I was in Pendragon as well! Those were some hot nights!

Drums and Dreams

Now then, I mentioned the 'production deal' a while ago, and this is what led to the conception of Shadowland, even if I did not realise at the time. The Cast had gone back into the studio to record some more demos. Our engineer (a guy called Robin), suggested that we really ought to try adding some drums and bass to a couple of them, because they were lacking something... 'But we're an electronic three piece' we automatically responded. But Robin was insistent that we tried... 'You don't have to use any of it' he said, knowing perfectly well where this was heading.

In came a couple of session guys... a drummer and a bassist. They listened to the songs a couple of times and then played along. A couple of takes later and it was done... and it was excellent!

Don't get me wrong, I am not saying the songs were excellent, but what they did just took everything up a notch and made me realise just how much I was missing the full band set up. I started to dream of the full rock band line up, and what could be possible. This was a defining moment, although things did not change straight away.

Dissent and Departures

The Cast gradually fell apart due to each of us having different ideas as to where we should be going. We had actually been offered a record deal – quite a momentous event for the band! Sadly, by then the cracks were already there, and we found ourselves arguing over the details of this deal, and the complexities of publishing and writing credits. That is never a good sign, and certainly not the way to enter into a new contract. Fortunately, we had the good sense to walk away from that offer (tempting though it was). Then we walked away from each other... it was nothing acrimonious, but we were all ready to move on.

Somehow, the other two had managed to leave, which left me tied up in that production deal. The problem was that the Soundmill guys wanted quality pop, and I was sliding rapidly back into prog! That deal was dissolved quite easily because the next song I wrote and wanted to demo was a song called 'Jigsaw', a ten-minute prog epic that really was not what these chaps wanted, and so we parted ways. Nevertheless, I loved my time with Soundmill, and it provided me with a very important part of my 'music business education'.

Forward and France

At this point I had joined forces with my long-term sparring partner, guitarist Karl Groom, although technically the band was still called The Cast.

We had met and formed a useful co-operative… my keyboards and computer stuff, combined with his eight-track recording gear. By now I had dispensed with the stand-alone drum machine and sequencer in favour of a thing called 'Pro 24' on an Atari computer. We started off by recording demos of 'Jigsaw', 'The Whistleblower' and a few others. The first two, of course, made it onto the debut Shadowland album, while others got dropped along the way.

Not long after we started collaborating, I managed to get a record deal with a label in Paris, France. I was armed with a more 'single-friendly' song called 'Walk on Water' as well as 'Jigsaw' and the other progressive numbers. Amazingly they were not scared off by the prog element.

Soon, we found ourselves in Paris, recording 'Walk on Water' for an intended single release. This session featured me (keyboards and vocals) and Karl (guitar and bass), along with Pendragon's Fudge Smith on drums. This was another great experience, and actually led to me doing other work at the studio in Paris, but our aspirations were somewhat dashed when France decided to appoint a 'minister of rock' who then decided that two thirds of French radio play should be in the French language.

Zut alors!

Bugger!

And so, this deal sank without trace.

Well, it is all part of that rich tapestry, and we did have fun while it lasted. We even got to film a video for 'Walk on Water'. We recruited Dave Wagstaffe as 'stunt drummer', because our French recording of this song featured programmed drums. I remember that day of filming very well – running through the song a hundred times on the increasingly muddy bank of the River Thames.

If I remember correctly, we eventually got shut down by some irritated neighbour who asked us to stop, but I am fairly confident that he knew this song a little too well by then!

At this stage, I was still using the name The Cast, but around that time, I concluded that the whole thing needed an upgrade, and a new name… I decided on Shadowland.

Deals and Debuts

Not long after the French deal finished, I had the opportunity to bring out an album with a new record company being set up off the back of a Dutch Fanzine called SI Music. Working within limited facilities and limited budget I wrote the first Strangers on a Train album, 'The Key'. This featured me, with Karl on guitars and Tracy Hitchings on vocals. If I ever put together a book of 'Strangers on a Train' lyrics, then there are many interesting anecdotes from that time.

But I digress… again! And we are so close now.

After 'The Key' release, I was asked to create a solo album for Tracy. I was really keen to get Shadowland off the starting blocks, so I came to an agreement with SI Music: I was to write an album for Tracy, and then we could do the Shadowland album.

That is what I did. We recorded and released 'From Ignorance to Ecstasy' in 1991, and then my path was clear to launch Shadowland.

And so, in 1992, Shadowland released its first album, 'Ring of Roses'. We followed this up with touring and two more studio albums, as well as a 'best of' album (with new material) and a DVD.

Collected here are all the lyrics as well as some of the background behind the songs, and a few anecdotes from the life and times of this band.

Although we have been inactive for a few years now, we have never 'split up' and as far as I am concerned, there might still be more to come from Shadowland, but for now, this book will hopefully offer a little added flavour to a band that specialised in nightmares, nonsense and nursery rhymes.

Ring of Roses

The debut album! This was one of the most exciting albums to release. It represented the culmination of a process of development that took place over quite a few years... from Sleepwalker, through The Cast to here! To me, this was all about learning to be a songwriter.

The Whistleblower

I'm blowing the whistle
On people I trusted before
I'm blowing the whistle
'Cos they can't be trusted anymore
The man in the white hat - He always wins in the end
He has a moral obligation - He's got a country to defend

I'm blowing the whistle
For freedom to find out the truth
I'm blowing the whistle
I'm coming down on the side of the youth
The man with the camera - He is coming round for tea
I can tell by the look in his eyes - That he's taken a picture of me

Light up the world - I'm coming home
In from the cold, so cold - I'm coming home - Light up the world

I'm blowing the whistle
On all the puppets surrounding me
I'm blowing the whistle
On all the strings we never see
The man with the suitcase - He is sitting in the park
He is looking for someone to trust
He's doing a balancing act in the dark!

Light up the world - I'm coming home
In from the cold, so cold - I'm coming home - Light up the world

Their secret world has put out all the light
The light of the ordinary world
So how can that be right?
There's a wreath by the side of the grave
There's a memory not to forget
It's like a secret service carpet
Where thousands of problems are swept!

Light up the world - I'm coming home
Light up the world - I'm coming home
In from the cold, so cold - I'm coming home - Light up the world

Behind the Lyric

This song has a very straightforward origin. I was watching a film called *The Whistle Blower*. It is a 1986 British spy film starring Michael Caine and a host of other familiar acting names. It is based on a novel of the same name by a writer called John Hale. There was something about the film that caught my attention, and, for me, it had some great lines in there. The lyric references to the 'man in the white hat' and 'their secret world has put out all the light' (amongst others) were plundered straight from the film (I have never read the book).

As you can see from the film title, 'The Whistleblower' should really be 'The Whistle Blower', but I never checked at the time, so it is what it is.

The 'Na na na' section at the end was simply inspired by my enjoyment of Michael Jackson songs!

Supplemental

This song has bags of energy and was always fun to perform live. It very often provided us with a powerful start to the set.

There was one time in Germany when we were just walking on to start this song... Mike Varty was playing keyboards by then. Someone had positioned the smoke machine rather strangely and he disappeared into his own personal fog of smoke. He had been complaining about a dodgy stomach just before going on stage and to be honest the rest of the band found this situation... amusing. Despite the fact that the music had started, it took me a while before I was able to deliver the first line of the song!

Jigsaw

There's an image in my head, but I can't make it whole
There's a picture in my mind - There's a story to be told
Just another anonymous part of a true-blue sky
Like a chameleon that's waiting for the fly

I'm living this life from the inside out
Can't understand what the whole thing's about
Keep a finger on the button now - That's the best I can do
And my eyes are wide for any hidden clues

Like pieces of a jigsaw, I'm falling apart again
I'm losing my way; do you know what I said?
I'm falling apart again
Like pieces of a jigsaw, I can't see the picture now
I'm losing my way, do you know what I said?
I can't see the picture now

I'm walking slowly
Don't want to step on the cracks
Got to find the missing pieces
I've got to fill all those gaps
I'm balancing the pros and the cons
I'm weighing up the right and the wrong
With the vestiges of sense still hanging on

Like pieces of a jigsaw, I'm falling apart again
I'm losing my way, do you know what I said?
I'm falling apart again
Like pieces of a jigsaw, I can't see the picture now
I'm losing my way, do you know what I said?
I can't see the picture now

I'm looking for the meaning of a nightmare
Beckoned to return by the face of beauty
I find myself ensnared
Tortured by some bitter cruelty!

I'm looking for the meaning of a dream
My heart is filled by the presence
Of someone special to me – someone special to me!
I'm looking for the meaning of a feeling
Emotion never felt before
Reaction unexpected
I'm living by the rules of an unknown law
I'm looking for the meaning of a memory
My heart is filled by the presence
Of someone special to me – someone special to me!

It's a one-way street
You can look behind, but you can't go back again
It's one-way street
You try standing still, but you can't remain the same!

I'm looking for the meaning of a language
I'm searching for a word in the dictionary
I find myself confused!
Believing in the reason of a missionary
I'm looking for the meaning of a nightmare –
My heart is filled with emptiness
As I fear for the presence
Of someone special to me

It's a one-way street
Don't try to recapture old memories
I've got to set my sights on a point in the distance
It's a one-way street
Going to pray that I take the right path
Before my memories just crumble into dust
Black and white dust yeah…

I'm lost in the wilderness
Like a tear in the rain
Like a piece of the jigsaw
Where the colours are the same
I'm lost in the wilderness

Like fear in the mist of pain
Like a piece of the jigsaw
Where the shapes are all the same
I'm drowning in the questions
Like a single passing thought
Like a piece of the jigsaw
Where the rules have not been taught
I'm drowning in the answers
Like a single grain of sand
And I hold the shattered world so tight in the palm of my hand
It's a one-way street...
It's a one-way street!
Perhaps there is someone else that I shall answer to one day
Perhaps I will see new colours emerging from the grey
There's something round the corner now
There's something very near!
The reason for my love
And the reason for my fear

Could I borrow more time?
Remember Dorian Gray?
But would I be prepared to pay the price
I know I'd have to pay?
There's something round the corner now
There's something very near!
The reason for my laughter
And the reason for my tears

Like pieces of a jigsaw, I'm falling apart again
I'm losing my way; do you know what I said?
I'm falling apart again
Like pieces of a jigsaw
I can't see the picture now
I'm losing my way; do you know what I said?
I can't see the picture now

Like pieces of a jigsaw, I'm falling apart again
I'm losing my way - do you know what I said?

I'm falling apart again
Like pieces of a jigsaw
I can't see the picture now
I'm losing my way; do you know what I said?
I can't see the picture no no no
It's a one-way street!

Just another anonymous part of a true-blue sky
Like a chameleon that's waiting for the fly
Like pieces of a jigsaw

Behind the Lyric

There are really two reasons for the existence of this song. I was tied into a 'production deal' at the time. As I mentioned in the introduction, the band was called 'The Cast', and we were creating what I would describe as 'pop-rock' songs.

However, I was getting disillusioned with our efforts to sound and look like Aha. I realised that it was time to return to the world of progressive rock.

Question: How do you get out of a pop deal?
Answer: Write a prog song.

Thus, Jigsaw was born. And I was free of the deal!

The second reason is a little more 'arty'. I had endured a series of vivid dreams, maybe four or five of them, where I was re-experiencing moments from my life, but they were distorted and meaningless. This song allowed me to try and make sense of myself once more; although now I read the lyrics again, I can see that I managed to keep that process fairly obscure!

Here are a couple of thoughts I can offer....

'Don't want to step on the cracks' – as a kid I used to avoid the cracks in the pavement like the plague. I am not sure why, but I considered the cracks to be bad luck.

'Beckoned to return by the face of beauty'...

I had a recurring nightmare where I am invited into a large black car by a beautiful woman... there is something familiar about her, like I know her, but I do not know exactly who it is...I know I should not give in and get into the car, but eventually I am tempted in... at which point she would change into some hideous, bloodthirsty demon.

'I'm lost in the wilderness, like a tear in the rain'...

This line was inspired by the speech that Rudger Hauer (playing a replicant) gives as the dying character Roy Batty in the film *Blade Runner*... His final line is 'All those moments will be lost in time... like tears in rain... Time to die'. A powerful image.

'Remember Dorian Gray?'...

This is more evidence of my obsession with eternal life and the corruption it can bring. Not long before writing 'Jigsaw' I wrote a song called 'Dorian Gray', inspired, of course, by the Oscar Wilde novel of the same name. This subject... the consequences of striving for eternal life... appears in quite a few of my songs. It also became the main theme of my first musical, 'She'.

Supplemental

This is one of my favourite Shadowland songs. We almost always played it as part of our live set list. I used to start at the piano singing, then take the microphone to the front and leave Mike Varty with the keyboards as the song progressed. The funny thing is that although in some ways 'Jigsaw' seems quite random and does not make clear sense... even to me... when I sang it, I felt that it made perfect sense... it was, as they say, an inner journey.

Scared of the Dark

I can hear a pin drop - I can hear a tear drop
Shattering like porcelain
Echoing a thousand cries for help
No running from these fears
Strange ideas from somewhere out in Half Moon Street
I face my darkest hour to meet my Nemesis again
My enemies again

"Hold my hand" - Don't let go!
"Take my arm" - Don't let go!
You and I will walk through fire
Deep into the Dead Zone

Crouching in the corners - Hiding in the shadows
They're moving through the garden
With knives oh they're aiming for me
"In the heart!" - I feel a hand on my arm
There's an unseen intruder
I can tell, I can hear echoes of
Laughter in the attic - Weeping in the hallway
You can't afford to panic
Has something just whispered my name?
From below! - Then the fear begins to grow
As a breath on my face says
"I know that you're scared of the dark!"

I can see faces looking through windows
Sneering at me - Peering in misery
The blood-stained glass - The mud stained glass?
Presents an inadequate mask for the features I see
The creatures I see
They're after my soul - My sanity
Ready to chase me all the way to hell and back
I'm under attack! Turn the light on – turn the light on!
Somewhere out in Half Moon Street
I'll play the game of hide and seek

Crouching in the corners - Hiding in the shadows
They're moving through the garden
With knives of they're aiming for me
"In the heart!" - I feel a hand on my arm
There's an unseen intruder
I can tell, I can hear echoes of
Laughter in the attic - Weeping in the hallway
You can't afford to panic
Has something just whispered my name?
From below!
Then the fear begins to grow
As a breath on my face says
"I know that you're scared of the dark!"
Scared of the dark!

It's raining, it's pouring, the old man's snoring
I can't get it out of my mind
No I can't shift it out of my mind
He went to bed and bumped his head
And never got up in the morning!
No, I can't get it out of my mind
No, I can't shift it out of my mind

Crouching in the corners - Hiding in the shadows
They're moving through the garden
With knives oh they're aiming for me
"In the heart!" - I feel a hand on my arm
There's an unseen intruder
I can tell, I can hear echoes of
Laughter in the attic - Weeping in the hallway
You can't afford to panic
Has something just whispered my name?
From below!
Then the fear begins to grow
As a breath on my face says
"I know that you're scared of the dark!"
Scared of the dark!

Behind the Lyric

This is another nightmare inspired song. It was actually an observation about how many horror films seemed to make it into my dreams. I used to watch a lot of horror films (I still do). *Half Moon Street* makes an appearance, which is another 'corruption of eternal life' story, and *The Dead Zone* is there. The 'laughter in the attic' segment is *Exorcist* inspired. The faces at the window reference is something that actually happened to me as a child. In the middle of the night a noise from outside woke me up, and I got up and opened the curtain. Pushed up against the glass was a face glaring back at me. A rather unpleasant surprise! It was probably a tramp, but by the time I had shouted the house down and turned on every light I could find, there was no sign of anyone.

Could I have imagined it?
I don't think so!

Nursery rhymes are also a theme that occurs a few times in the Shadowland material. I consider them to be wonderfully dark little poems that manage to reach out a clawed hand deep into our subconscious.

Supplemental

For such a relatively short song, there are quite a few lyrics in this song. It was during the Shadowland tours that I developed my ability to 'sing in Chinese', thus enabling me to navigate such songs as 'Scared of the Dark'.

Naturally, it is not really Chinese, and I apologise to the Chinese people for my inaccurate representation of their mother tongue. Basically, it is the ability to sing complete and utter nonsense in the absence of the correct words. This is a skill I admired very much in a singer I had worked with around that time, Damian Wilson, who had truly perfected this ability to the point that he could sing a whole song 'in Chinese' and you would walk away feeling like you understood precisely what he was singing about. I do not profess to have mastered it to that extent, but I must admit, it has got me out of a few tight corners over the years.

Painting by Numbers

Painting by numbers
I'm looking for colours
Painting by numbers
I'm looking for colours
Don't find another one
I've only just begun

Ooh - You make me want to know you!
Ooh - You make me want to hold you!

I'm waiting - I'm waiting for a sign
A sign of hope or confidence
I'm searching - For what the picture means to me
Greater understanding - The more there is to see

I'm waiting - I'm waiting for a clue
A clue to identity
And I'm searching for honesty or lies
Go on taking views, or taking sides

Ooh - You make me want to know you!
Ooh - You make me want to hold you!

I'm running - I'm running to the goal
With the weight upon my shoulder
All shivering with cold
I'm falling - I'm falling to the ground
A grey and faded memory
A long forgotten sight - A long forgotten sound

Blue! The colour flooding through me
As you left me on my own
To watch the world go by - Pass me by!

Yellow is the jealousy
A self-destructive energy

That always took a grip on me
It follows me around
A saffron shadow hand
Beating at the door

Looking at my life: "A rose tinted spectacle"
Justified experiences so coloured and respectable
The light's too bright to let the truth come in again
Don't lock me in a cell - Don't throw away the key!
I've got no ground to stand on
No company but me!

Painting by numbers
I'm looking for colours
Don't find another one
I've only just begun it

Painting by numbers
I'm looking for colours
Don't find another one
I've only just begun

Behind the Lyric

I was looking at a magazine in some waiting room. It contained a large picture that you were supposed to stare at and see images in. It was not one of those 'magic eye 3D' ones, but along those lines. I stared and saw all sorts of things… just not what I was supposed to see!

Supplemental

I like this song, but I felt it was weaker than the others, particularly when we played it live. I could see in the audience that it was the song where people decided to go and grab a beer or nip off to the toilet. You notice these things from the stage!

Hall of Mirrors

Here I stand - Surrounded by these old reflections
Faces of my past!
Shadows everlasting, etched in the glass
Is there nothing I can do, nothing I can say
To make it all come true
Then it's all over now? Yes, it's all over now!

This dance has got to end - I always knew it would
This dance has got to end
I never understood the message
The message in the mirrors... The mirrors?
Is there no one else to blame? No one else to hate?
So it's all over now? Yes, it's all over now!

Here I lie, fever on my brow
And all that I believed has ceased to be the truth
I thought I'd found again
Like the Paradiso fantasy, it's always coming back to me
Put your fate in the hands of a thousand judges!
I'm painting a picture, looking in a mirror
That's flesh and blood - That's heart and soul!
I'm painting a picture - Looking in a mirror
Which of me is real?
Which of you is false beyond redemption?

Am I the hero? He never takes the fall
Leaving all his failings so secure behind the door
Am I the hero? Expecting all the prizes
Taking up the challenge of perfection
Such distinction... Determination... Seduction?
Someone out there knows that's what I need to be!
You're what I'd die for!
You're what I lied for so easily!

Dear "Jane" - So quick to criticise
And ready to condemn the actions, the attitudes

"The obvious deceit of all such men"!
Dear "John" Just lives to put me down again
He does it for the best
He operates to safeguard and protect all his brethren!

Bleeding feet and bleeding hands
I'm standing on a pedestal, ankle deep in broken glass
Broken faith... Hope gone past... Fallen grace!
Bleeding feet and bleeding hands
I'm standing on a pedestal, ankle deep in broken glass
Broken faith... Hope gone past... Fallen grace!

Je suis le chevalier sans chevalle!
Je suis le chevalier sans chevalle!

Would it shock you to know with your moralized hypocrisy
Your patronizing jealousy
That I couldn't give a damn?
I could wait forever - I could wait for even longer
I can feel the envy in your heart
And that just makes me stronger

It's that one way street again - But did I take the right path?
It's that one-way street again
But did I make those choices too fast?
Can you throw the first stone? Are you really without sin?
Can you cast that first stone
And destroy all the memories and meanings?

So I look into the mirrors
A multitude of characters all to call my own
There's a Jekyll, there's a Hyde
Changing moon a changing tide
You must have seen - You must have known
I can hold them all together
With a common aim - A common cause
Different rules, different laws
You can say that I'm the one to blame

But maybe you're the same
But maybe you're the same
Here I stand - Surrounded by these old reflections
Faces of my past - Surrounded by these old reflections

And this dance has got to end - It always had to end
You know it had to end
How can you say that I'm to blame?
'Cause maybe you're the same
I know you are the same - No change!

Behind the Lyric

"Mirrors,' she said, 'are never to be trusted."

Neil Gaiman

Shadowland were always at their best using dark images. The nursery rhyme, the nightmare and in this case the fairground... something else I, for one, find a disturbing place! The hall of mirrors seemed a great environment to explore the effect of key people and situations in my life. I use it to question some of the choices I made and their potential effect on my life. Threaded through the song are some references that people might recognise...

'Paradiso fantasy' of course refers to the Paradiso venue in Amsterdam, Holland. Some of my most pivotal gig experiences happened there; it was an unforgettable place to play, although I sadly have not played there for quite a while.

'Dear Jane' was someone I encountered years ago who was helping with my musical journey at the time. It soon became clear that she had a negative attitude to almost everything I offered or suggested, so I chose to go off and do everything she told me not to!

My reference to Jekyll and Hyde is one of the first times I reveal my passion for the Victorian Era. This would only grow over time!

Supplemental

This was always one of our more popular live numbers. There were lots of words to remember, which was never great news for me. I remember before one gig I was particularly nervous about remembering these lyrics. So, I wrote a load of key words and triggers on a piece of paper and put it on the stage floor next to my set list. The only problem was that when I came out for the show, I saw that it had disappeared! I then spent the duration of the first half of the set worrying I would not remember the words. I did in fact make it through, which was a relief, but what really got to me was, after the gig, a guy came up to me and asked me to sign that missing lyric sheet! I got my revenge though... I spelled my name wrong!

The Kruhulick Syndrome

Supplemental

This is an instrumental, and one of the very few 'abstract' pieces of music I have written... I am almost always driven by images or stories. Once it was recorded, we needed a name for this piece. Karl and I had been talking about the film *The Seven Year Itch* starring Marilyn Monroe, and we both particularly remembered the janitor character. After asking around, we finally re-discovered his name.... Mr Kruhulick - what a great name!

And so 'The Kruhulick Syndrome' was born.

Ring of Roses

Dance around in circles
Call me by another name
See the mark of roses on your skin
Call me by another name
Holding hands again!
Holding hands again!

Leading all the dancing fools
Watching them ignore the rules
They fought so hard to make!
Like stepping-stones across the water
See the blind man jumping from mistake to mistake!
Singing as they run around
And laughing as they all fall down again
There's danger in the game they play
So call him by another name
Holding hands - We're holding hands again!

Caught in a ring of roses
Got to stay on my feet - Don't let it deceive me
Caught in a ring of roses
Got to leave it to fate - Don't hesitate

Following the dancing children
Pull the wool right down across their innocent wide eyes!
I see the mark of roses
It's painted on with colours from an endless flow of lies!
Is someone there misguiding me
Dealing insecurity like poison from a smile?
There's danger in the game they play
So call him by another name
Holding hands - We're holding hands again!

Caught in a ring of roses
Got to stay on my feet - Don't let it deceive me
Caught in a ring of roses

Got to leave it to fate - Don't hesitate
(Come face to face with my life)
I'm running round in circles now
I'm dancing round in circles now

Behind the Lyric

It is probably not hard to guess the origin of this song. It is another nursery rhyme, but the belief was that it was sung by children from the time of the plague.

The most well-known verse was…

Ring-a-ring o' roses,
A pocket full of posies,
A-tishoo! A-tishoo!
We all fall down.

It was believed that the 'roses' represented the red marks or lesions that appeared on the body as a symptom of the plague.

The 'pocket full of posies' referred to the use of herbs and flowers as a way to protect against the disease by using natural perfume. 'A-tishoo' was simply the sneeze that often heralded the start of the illness.

'We all fall down' speaks for itself!

I have since learned that in fact it is very unlikely this rhyme originated from the time of the plague, but nevertheless, I find the imagery beguiling.

Supplemental

The 12-minute version! During the 'Lurv Ambassadors' tour that Shadowland did with that marvellous band, Jadis, we had to travel back from Berlin all the way to Tilburg in Holland, for the next gig. This meant a gruelling overnight drive in a very uncomfortable minibus. We arrived outside the venue and waited for it to open, since we could not yet check into our hotel. Everyone was extremely tired, and somehow, we had to make it through a day of unloading gear, setting up and sound checking, and of course the show. My personal solution was to drink plenty of caffeine. However, not being a coffee drinker, I decided to drink lots of coke. Through some strange twist of logic, I decided that was too sweet, unless I added Jack Daniels. The venue had kindly presented us with a couple of bottles! Everyone else had similar solutions!

I have never walked on stage affected by alcohol… except this gig! I have never done that since… but on this one occasion I 'floated' through the gig. I suspect I was not alone, because we finished the set as usual with 'Ring of Roses'… always a fun song that people could join in with. For some reason (I blame Mr. Daniels), our rendition that night went on for about 12 minutes! Members of Jadis joined us on stage and somehow we seemed incapable of stopping, so round and round that chorus we went! It all seemed terrific on stage, but I must assume the audience thought we had gone mad…

We performed 'Ring of Roses' as part of a set for a band we put together, called Neo. The idea of the band was to play a selection of songs connected to the musicians in the band. In this case we were playing a varied set, including Pendragon (Nick Barrett and myself), IQ (Andy Edwards, John Jowitt), Pallas (Alan Reed) and Shadowland (myself). Rehearsals were entertaining, if only because we could not resist finding humour in most of the songs we were playing. 'Ring of Roses' came under fire when John Jowitt thought I was singing 'holding Hans again' instead of 'holding hands again'. Initially, I kind of ignored this joke, but sadly, it grew on me as time went past.

By the time we stood on stage at the ROSFest festival in America, this proved to be a real problem. I remember having to focus on some patch of dirt on the stage just to get past that bit… thanks John!

Through the Looking Glass

This is the second Shadowland album. This was important to me, because it proved that this band was not just a one album novelty. All the music featured was written specifically for the album, whereas 'Ring of Roses' had partly developed out of earlier projects.

We wanted the cover to have a suitably surreal vibe, and we ran with the idea of setting up loads of shop dummy bits and pieces in a field. It made for an interesting day out!

A Matter of Perspective

Looking for reason
On a far distant plane
Trying to tie the loose ends
Together again

Keeping perspective
On a colourful thought
With feet on the ground
Or that's what the grey men
Have taught

Holding a moment
Just one second more
It's something I touched
That I touched in a dream once before
Don't let them guide me anymore...

It's all in the mind
It's all in the mind
Scattered in every direction
It's part of the grandest design
It's all in the mind
Oh so easy to find
Shattering signs and restrictions
It's part of the grandest design
It's all in the mind

Behind the Lyric

This song has a simple explanation. I wrote a song called 'Mindgames' for this album, but I wanted something light and vulnerable to begin the album before the relative fury of 'The Hunger'. It occurred to me that some kind of 'Mindgames' prelude would work well here, and then we would get the full version later.

Supplemental

Ah, so many anecdotes with this one! But I will tell you the one that I have told many times before… mostly at 'house gigs'.

It happened when Shadowland appeared at the Wyspiański Theatre in Katowice, Poland. We were there to record our show for a DVD, and I decided it would make a great start to the set if we began with 'Perspective' and then powered into 'The Hunger' – lots of drama.

It would be even more dramatic if we closed the theatre curtains and started the gig with just myself, and Mark Westwood on acoustic guitar. We could walk out in front of the curtain, and busk our way through the opening segment, before the big bass note kicks in and the curtain flies open, revealing the rest of the band ready to surge into the opening frenetic number, 'The Hunger'.

What could possibly go wrong?
Well, I'll tell you!

The audience was in… sat down… the front curtain was closed… the lights went down… there was an expectant buzz around the auditorium. Mark was at the side of the stage with me, and we were preparing to go on and start the gig. Mark was all plugged in and ready. It was then we noticed that I had forgotten my radio mic! Ouch! Paddy Darlington (crew member) dashed back round to the stage and grabbed my microphone, then ran back and handed it to me… finally we were ready to go!

Mark went on first. He started strumming the opening chords as he walked confidently onto the stage in front of the curtain.

Then, it all went into slow motion!

I was following Mark onto stage, and I could immediately see that we might have a problem. His guitar lead was trailing behind him, as it should have, but in this case, it was slowly (or not so slowly) coiling around the bass pedals. And then I could see it getting tighter and tighter as Mark continued to walk forward. In reality this all happened quickly and there was no time for me to stop him or fix the situation.

Inevitably he reached the point of no return, and the sumptuous, rich, amplified sound of his acoustic was suddenly reduced to a feeble twang, as the lead sprang out of its socket on the guitar. We both froze on stage as Mark did a rather Monty Python double take as he realised what had happened.

By this time the audience was beginning to see the funny side, as Mark slowly leant down and picked up the lead… then slowly plugged the guitar in. Why we did everything 'slowly' I have no idea – maybe we hoped the audience would not notice! Below there is a rather blurred picture which nevertheless captures the two of us as we launch into the song, after the lead incident.

I leant over to him and said, 'don't worry, we'll edit it later'… then he started playing again, and we did the song.

I remember thinking 'Ok, so we've had the big mess up… the rest of the show should be fine'…. Famous last words!

The Hunger

A master of disguise
You live beyond mundane survival
A force without reflection
Let the blood start flowing over me
Dragging out the need that takes them by surprise
Before the hate just smothers them
And all that's left are ghosts and cries

You laugh to take away the fear of drowning
You sing to lead us all to such temptation

Don't try to hide - There's emptiness behind those eyes
It's a matter of time
Before this army tears away your lies

You've got no hold on me
Scream and shout your cold frustration
I'm not your fantasy
There is nothing you can do about it

You're here by invitation - Part of this community
Hypnotic conversation; drawing in your victims
I can see they're following a path
That takes them to the edge - A fragile ledge
Addiction is the slender rope they balance on
It's lost and hopeless

You cry to bring us all to sympathy and guilt
Don't try to hide - There's emptiness behind those eyes

You've got no hold on me
Scream and shout your cold frustration
I'm not your fantasy
There is nothing you can do about it
You've got no hold on me
You can rage until hell freezes over

I'm not your vanity
There is nothing here for you at all

Don't try to hide
There's emptiness behind those eyes
It's a matter of time
Before you're pulled
Right across that deadly line...

You've got no hold on me
Scream and shout your cold frustration
I'm not that fantasy
There is nothing you can do about it
You've got no hold on me
You can rage until hell freezes over
I'm not your vanity
There is nothing here for you at all
You've got no hold on me
Curse the fate that guides your actions
I'm not your guarantee
There is nothing you can do about it
You've got no hold on me
You can fight against your own reactions
I'm not your sanity
There is nothing here for you at all
There is nothing here for you at all
There is nothing here for you at all

Behind the Lyric

"You're a part of me now and I cannot let you go."

Miriam Blaylock in *The Hunger*

Every now and then you meet someone who has an intensely disruptive effect on the people around them. Everything becomes a drama, way out of proportion… or a conspiracy. When something goes wrong, it is never their fault, but they are quick to blame someone else. Through all of this they still carry enough charisma to ensure there are people who will support them… at least for a while.

The Hunger was a vampire film, and I wanted to write this song about a 'social vampire'.

Supplemental

After the fiasco at the start of the Shadowland gig in Poland, what else could possibly go wrong?
Well, I'll tell you!

The plan: Low bass note growling around the theatre… smoke… swirling lights… the curtain opens revealing the rest of the band… Mark and I quickly take up our on stage 'band positions'… there is a drum cue… the band powers into the 'The Hunger', and I provide a commanding rendition of the vocals to provide the audience with a confident and blistering start to the show!

The reality: The low note growled around the theatre… there was smoke… and swirling lights… the curtain opened, revealing the rest of the band… Mark and I quickly took up our positions… drum cue… band started!

So, what was the problem?
Well, I'll tell you!

As I have mentioned a few times now, remembering lyrics is not exactly my superpower. For this particular tour, I had set up my laptop as an autocue, and we simply popped that at the front of the stage, usually hidden in a 'false monitor speaker'. I had a little white remote control in the pocket of my long black coat (for this was the uniform of Shadowland), which would enable me to move the programme through the pages... simple. We had already performed several gigs and this method had worked very well!

Until this night!

As the curtain opened, I dived into my position behind the mic stand and looked down at the screen to be sure it was on the right song. Sadly, it was on no song... just a blank screen! I furiously pressed the remote control in my pocket (which in itself must have looked a little strange), but to no avail.

I could hear the intro music racing its way inexorably towards verse one... a bit like those steam trains in the silent movies, with the girl tied to the rail... So, I quickly edged myself off stage and shouted to Paddy... 'Fix that bleedin' laptop!'. I think he had already spotted the problem and without hesitation he ran on stage and planted himself cross-legged in front of the laptop at the front of the stage. People in the audience must have been mystified by what he was doing there. He remained very calm about it all, and it looked like he was doing a bit of online banking!

Meanwhile, I was clinging on for dear life as I did my best to deliver the first verse. I was pretty sure I could get as far as the end of the first chorus, and then things were going to get sticky. I was just preparing to descend into a series of mumbled lines (yes, folks... 'singing in Chinese'), when Paddy nodded at me and casually left the stage. My lyrics were back... phew!

And finally, everything was on track with the gig. If you happen to have the DVD 'Edge of Night', watch very carefully at the start of the show, and despite some brilliant editing, you will catch a glimpse of Mr Patrick Darlington during his 'laptop fixing' mission.

Dreams of the Ferryman

I'm smothered by my pillow
Heavy eyelids pin me down now
With insane confidence
He guides me through the sleeping windows
He leaves two wishes on her eyes
One for the tears - And one for the cries of, screams of…

'Mercy, please don't do this to me - Let this be my nightmare
Far beyond the real world - Just another dream'

He stands on blood red dirt
And smiles behind his vulgar mask
Of animals and clowns
Safe in mother's hand me downs
Crying for a tortured mind
With fairy tales and candy lies
This wolf in sheep's disguise
Can see me clearly…

'Mercy, please don't do this to me - Let this be my nightmare
Far beyond the real world - Just another dream'

The slightest breath away
He crows in rancid whispers
'I've beaten you again
You lose to me once more
Tempted by my siren's call'
He leaves two wishes on her eyes
One for the tears - And one for the cries of, screams of…

'Mercy, please don't do this to me - Let this be my nightmare
Far beyond the real world - Just another dream'

Let me return to the still and the dark of untroubled sleep
Where the will and the heart of all mankind is undefeated

He knows my name - There's nowhere else to hide
He knows my name - Two wishes on her eyes!
He knows my name - There's nowhere else to hide
He knows my name - Two wishes on her eyes!

Behind the Lyric

This is probably the most Shadowland of Shadowland tracks! It is also one of my absolute favourite songs that I wrote for this band.

Sensitivity warning! If you are not keen on horror images, or have a sensitive disposition, then maybe you should skip this next paragraph…

It all began with a recurring dream… more of a nightmare really. I would find myself on some patch of deserted moorland, filled with a sense of danger. It is night-time but there is always a bright moon. I start walking in search of other people, or even a sign of civilization… houses or a small village, perhaps.

Before long, I trip over a body. This is the victim of the 'Ferryman' - a serial killer, whom I believe is hunting me right now. There are coins on the eyes of the mutilated prey. Now, I can hear noises a little way away, and it is clear that the 'Ferryman' is stalking me. I scramble away in an attempt to gain some distance from this invisible enemy. Suddenly I see the headlights of a car and realise that I am not far away from a road, so I run in that direction, hoping to get help. Sadly, I trip over another mutilated body, again with coins on the eyes. I watch as the car continues along the road and disappears. I hear laughing in the distance behind me.

This game of cat and mouse continued across several dreams, over a period of years. Then the story moved forward suddenly…

I find myself back on the moorland, standing next to another victim, but something has changed… It is as if I am hunting the Ferryman instead of him hunting me. I reach the road and follow it until I can see lights. It is a small hotel. I check into this hotel and discover that there are four other people currently staying there. After hearing a familiar laugh, I realise without doubt (as often happens in dreams) that one of the guests must be the Ferryman. I now know I can capture this killer, and I go to my hotel room to prepare a plan of action…

Then I woke up!

I remember telling some friends about this latest development in the story and was advised that it would make a great song, so that is what I did – I wrote 'Dreams of the Ferryman'.

The frustrating thing is, I am still waiting for the next dream, so I can find out exactly who the killer is!

Supplemental

Not only was this one of my favourite Shadowland tracks, but this also proved to be an audience favourite as well. It was considered by most to be the definitive Shadowland track!

I think now is the best time to mention the 'Mark Westwood Serial Killer Theory'... We were sitting in a pub before one of the gigs, discussing the Ferryman song. Mark announced that all serial killers seemed to come with three names...

'For example, John Wayne Gacy', said Mark.

'Interesting', said Clive. 'Can you give some other examples?'

'Well', said Mark after a pause, 'there's Randy Steven Kraft and Derrick Todd Lee'.

'Ok, good' said Clive, 'and just to really seal this theory, just one more?'

Mark sat for a moment thinking. Then, after a pensive sip of his beer he announced, 'how about Jack THE Ripper?'.

Half Moon Street

Go right home where you Daddy's waiting for you
Go right home where your family is safe behind the wall
Run right back - Put your hand against the door
(Hard against the door)
Lie right down - Keep your eyes upon the floor

I wait for the dawn to come
Am I safe from the man with hatred in his eyes?
Still look for the morning sun
He's part of the world - He's part of the shadow lies
I wait for the day to come
There's fear in the heart of the child as the mother cries
Still pray for the morning sun
He's scared of the dark - He's scared of the shadow lies, lies, lies!

Never trust a man who hides behind a suit
Or an angry politician with an ozone friendly attitude
You've got to go right home - Don't hang around too late
You've got to go right home - Don't be afraid...

Never trust a man who hides behind a crowd
Or a safety net philosopher accusing you of being proud
You've got to run right back - Don't stay away too late
You've got to lie right down - Don't be afraid...

I wait for the dawn to come
Am I safe from the man with hatred in his eyes?
Still look for the morning sun
He's part of the world - He's part of the shadow lies
I wait for the day to come
There's fear in the heart of the child as the mother cries
Still pray for the morning sun
He's scared of the dark - He's scared of the shadow lies, lies, lies!

I wait for the dawn to come
Let the bitter tears of blood run from his eyes

Still look for the morning sun
He's got to escape from the misery of lies
I wait for the day to come
Am I safe from the man with hatred in his eyes?
Still pray for the morning sun
He's part of the world - He's part of the shadow lies

Behind the Lyric

"I'll share your madness because there's grandeur in it."
                    Eve Brandon in *The Man in Half Moon Street*

This is a song of paranoia. I remember having flu (the real one, not 'man flu'), and a high temperature. While I had this fever I was in and out of sleep, and some of the time, with all the weird dreams and thoughts I was having, I could not tell whether I was awake or asleep.

The title 'Half Moon Street' comes from the name of a 1945 horror film called *The Man in Half Moon Street* about a scientist who has found a way to prolong life... naturally things go badly for the scientist!

Supplemental

Because of the added rhythmic and sequenced elements in this song, we actually used a very primitive backing track. It was something very basic, recorded onto a cassette, with the track sounds on the right and the click track for Nick Harradence (drums) on the left. Nick would just wear headphones for this song, lean over and grab the Walkman (yes, indeed!) and press play.

Primitive or not, it worked.

When the World Turns to White

So many lies, misconceptions and signs
Like fingerprints at the scene of a crime
This is our prize, our black legacy
The brooding thoughts of an untamed mind
Falling, crying...

Dress the old world in diamonds and dreams
Wipe darkness away - Let the innocent breathe
It is clean and virgin - Free from guilt
And the sins of our fathers
The sins of our lives
The sins of our fathers
The sins of our lives

I can see it - But it's only there when I close my eyes to you
I can see it - But it's only real when they hide me from the truth
The blanket is stretched over jealousy, over greed
Hard, genuine honesty; never touched, never seen
Bleeds into those darkest corners - Reaches to the night
With my mind sharply focused
I can watch you create a new life

Conciliatory promises - Keeps those feelings at bay
A verbal preventative medicine
Made for the moment - Saving the day
Creeps into those secret places
Reaches to the light
From the farthest shores and islands
I can watch the world turn to white

Keeping one step ahead
Staying one step behind
I can go on reading the warnings and threats
They're hidden between all the lines
Forced into conscious thought
Dragged into sight

Disregarding ancient laws
I can watch the world turn to white

I can see it - But it's only there
When I close my eyes to you
I can see it - But it's only real
When they hide me from the truth
I can see it - But it's only there
When I close my eyes to you

When the world turns to white
There's an end to the bruises and scars
And the fear in your heart
When the world turns to white
There's an end to corruption of time
And the fall of mankind

When the world turns to white
We forget the insatiable craving
For hatred and lies
When the world turns to white
We forget that the
Primeval yearning for violence
Is rising again

I can see it - But it's only there
When I close my eyes to you
I can see it - But it's only real
When they hide me from the truth

I can see it - But it's only there
When I close my eyes to you
I can see it - But it's only real
When they hide me from the truth

I can see it
I can see it

Behind the Lyric

"The snow was endless, a heavy blanket on the outdoors; it had a way about it. A beauty. But I knew that, like many things, beauty could be deceiving."

Cambria Hebert

I love snow... there has never been enough of it in my life. I remember when I was a very young child, it had snowed each winter, so one year my parents bought me a toboggan for Christmas... it never snowed there again for the rest of my childhood – I kid you not!

What I loved about snow as a child, was that it seemed to cover all the imperfections on the ground – it was like a fresh start... then there were also snowballs, snowmen and generally sliding around!

For a little while, the snow hid the truth.

Supplemental

This song was only in our set list for a few gigs. I remember one night being interviewed after the show, and the guy asked me why I felt the need to write a racist song? I was shocked at the question and asked him which song. He answered, 'When the World Turns to White'. I could not believe it! It took me a while to explain and prove to him that this song was about nothing more than snow. Nevertheless, I took it out of the set list from that point on!

It is also worth pointing out that I dragged my violin out for the first time in years just to do the violin solo in this track. I felt like a total beginner again, and it took me several days to manage what I did record in the end. Since then, when I need real violin in the studio, I get my old university pal, Penny Gee, to pop in and record... much better!

The Waking Hour

The phantom of the opera lives in a tortured world
Of make believe and love
Uncovers a truth that hurts so much to her
A prisoner
The lost survivor of the human race
Search in despair for another soul
To face this empty kind of loneliness

There's a photo on your wall
I wonder why it's there
A well protected message
A secret world affair
A traveller has rested from his journey here before
You might have known me then
But you can't be sure

I see you lying naked in the sun
I watch your body burn into the dust
I stand alone with nothing left to see
As the anger of the dawn - It starts pouring over me
I'm drowning in the blood red sea
Can't touch your skin - No longer feeling anything
Fading fast - Nothing lasts beyond the waking hour...

A victim of suspicion
Sentenced to eternity
With no defence o trust
Wanders through the self-inflicted halls of pain
Lost again
I can follow you across these dreams
Reaching out to hidden doorways

All I need is time to guide you through to me
There's a meaning in your smile
And a force behind your touch
I try to understand, but there's never quite enough

A traveller has rested from his journey here before
You might have known me then, but you can't be sure

I see you lying naked in the sun
I watch your body burn into the dust
I stand alone with nothing left to see
As the anger of the dawn - It starts pouring over me
I'm drowning in the blood red sea
Can't touch your skin - No longer feeling anything
Fading fast - Nothing lasts beyond the waking hour...

There's a letter in your hand
I wonder why it's there
A private invitation - A secret world affair
A traveller has rested from his journey here before
You might have known me then, but you can't be sure

I see you lying naked in the sun
I watch your body burn into the dust
I stand alone with nothing left to see
As the anger of the dawn - It starts pouring over me
I'm drowning in the blood red sea
Losing my grip - No longer holding anything
Fading fast - Nothing lasts beyond the waking hour...

I see you lying naked in the sun
I watch your body burn into the dust
I stand alone with nothing left to see
As the anger of the dawn - It starts pouring over me
I'm drowning in the blood red sea
Can't touch your skin - No longer feeling anything
Fading fast
Nothing lasts
Beyond the waking hour...

Behind the Lyric

William Shakespeare, *Macbeth*

There are some lyrics I have written that make very little sense to me anymore. All I can remember about this song is that I woke up at 4am one night and wrote most of these words. I remember hearing that four in the morning was often referred to as the 'waking hour', and I always used to find that this was the time of night where it felt like you were the only person awake... the whole world is asleep... apart from just you!

As a child this thought used to terrify me, but later in life I found it a comforting idea... bearing in mind, of course, that it is never true!

Supplemental

This track has a fairly strong vampire theme to it and is one of quite a few songs I have written about vampires. The Arena number, 'Don't Forget to Breathe' is another good example. I am a big fan of all the classic horror film monsters – Frankenstein's monster, vampires, mummies, zombies and so on. They are an excellent source of analogy in lyric writing. I am not so keen on the way that many of these creatures have been over-romanticised in recent years, but it seems that things have to be more saccharine nowadays.

Anyway... I digress... again!

Through the Looking Glass

There's a man in paper bags
His ticket's worth a thousand pounds
Can you hear him?
Small voice, small sound
Thinking costs a thousand pounds
Can you hear him?
Lost voice, lost sound

"Look for the wood in the trees, my friend"
"Look for the fish in the sea"...
(There's plenty more where they came from)

There's a king, he's painted white
Can you see him - foolish leader
For his crown, he let them fight
Do you know this foolish leader?
He cut off his nose despite his face
He failed in his quest for a better place...

Running around in a state of delirium
Burning it up to the point of oblivion
I could reason with big black dots
Give the meaning in big round words
But no one ever heard me
No one ever heard me

Alice, Alice - Tell me what you meant by this
Alice, Alice - Show me what you meant by this

Let the search begin for
The Eighth Wonder of the World
Go look before
The Hanging Gardens fall down
Beyond the Temple of Dian
Just rubble and dust
Nothing lasts forever

Nothing lasts forever

There's a girl, she understands
"Hold me tight now, don't let go now"
She listens hard and holds my hand
Where can she be, now that I'm alone?

Alice, Alice - Alice, Alice

It's been a long day - Such a hard day
Lying around, waiting for the ground
To open up and swallow you whole
Like some human antidote
To the poison of the world
Listen to the bastard scream
You'd have thought that he's never been heard

It's been a cruel turn - A twist of the knife
As you're pushed and pushed
Towards the precipice of life
Look at the boys again - Can you really be so sure
Who the sniper is?
So can you really take much more of this?

Don't look at me - With your dark warning eyes
Cutting through my skull as you try to read my mind
You'll never get back – Get back what you're looking for
Not in a million years
You will hypnotise no more - No more!

Don't look back – Don't look back
You are part of this one way street
Don't let go - Don't let go
No surrender, no defeat
When you talk to me with dialing tones
There's no disguise, I've always known
Your thoughts can travel far
And there's no denying what they are

Let me find another path - Another dream
This is a false kind of universe - It's not what it seems...

Alice, Alice - You made my future with your kiss
Alice, Alice - Tell me what you meant by this

Through the looking glass - I see you staring back at me
Through the looking glass - I know just what you did to me

Alice, Alice - You sealed my future with your kiss
Alice, Alice - Show me what you meant by this...

Behind the Lyric

"I knew who I was this morning, but I've changed a few times since then."
Lewis Carroll, *Alice in Wonderland*

I was channelling Lewis Carroll for this song. As a matter of fact, the images conjured up by this author seem to me to suit Shadowland down to the ground, which is why I chose to make this song the title of the album as well.

This whole song is veiled in a kind of nonsense verse whilst at the same time I use this framework to remember the 'ups and downs' of a friend from university and the possible path that drugs might take you.

Supplemental

This was a challenging but satisfying song to perform live. I have one amusing memory regarding this song. Bear with me on this one…

At one gig we played – I cannot remember where we were – five guys (actually four males and a female – I shall collectively call them 'guys') turned up, all wearing white baseball caps. Each one of them had a large capital letter written on it in thick black marker pen. You could certainly see the letter from quite a distance. They were constantly waving at me and pointing at their hats as I sang from the stage. Then, I got it. In the order they were standing, their hats spelt out the word A L I C E. This was a very nice little tribute to the 'Through the Looking Glass' song. The guys pretty much stood to attention in this order in anticipation of the band playing the song, which we indeed did. The moment came, and the letters on their caps became totally relevant with the chorus of…

'Alice, Alice
You made my future with your kiss' etc.

Once the song was played, the girl obviously decided her work was done, and she fell back towards the bar, leaving her friends who were clearly enjoying the show very much. This was fine, of course, but she had been wearing the cap with the 'A' on it, and all I could see from stage for the remainder of the gig was the word 'LICE'… hard to ignore!

Mindgames

They say "The meek shall inherit the earth"
Small compensation for a question of birth
I've got a strong feeling, but it's dying away
Some confirmation of a slightly unusual day

They'll take you by kindness - They'll take you by force
And promise the world that it's all in a very good cause
Then take a bow and wait for the fools to applaud

A silhouette waves from a light on the wall
Don't look down now 'cause you're likely to fall
Playing their games in the wink of an eye
Don't let them lead you
Don't let them teach you to fly

Clutching a handful of roses and thorns
I follow the dance, and I dance to the drums and the horns
Part of the spirit that rises and falls

It's all in the mind - It's all in the mind
Scattered in every direction
It's part of the grandest design
It's all in the mind – Oh so easy to find
Shattering signs and restrictions
It's part of the grandest design
It's all in the mind...

There on the ground is a small jigsaw piece
Waiting to make my picture complete
But the image is covered with blood from my hands
The violence of ages - I can see it inherent in man
Falling asleep - It's a last desperate defence
Too much is real, but nothing that makes any sense
These could be meanings for all the rest

It's all in the mind - It's all in the mind

Scattered in every direction
It's part of the grandest design
It's all in the mind – Oh so easy to find
Shattering signs and restrictions
It's part of the grandest design

Unconscious cause
A ballad half sung
Bitter sweet taste
And it's there on the tip of my tongue
These could be dreams for anyone...

It's all in the mind - It's all in the mind
Scattered in every direction
It's part of the grandest design
It's all in the mind – Oh so easy to find
Shattering signs and restrictions
It's part of the grandest design
It's all in mind!

Behind the Lyric

This is the full version of the opening song 'A Matter of Perspective'. For the most part this is a fairly gentle song about losing a hold on reality... it gets a little darker towards the end.

Several of these lines refer to vague childhood memories: half remembered images that do not really make sense anymore.

'A silhouette waves from a light on the wall' refers to one time when my dad entertained me with shadows on the wall. He sat me down and told me not to turn around, and I was delighted to witness an array of primitive hand shadow puppets on the wall – rabbit, snail, swan etc. But suddenly something 'magical' happened and the shadow on the wall transformed into a full standing image of what looked like Bugs Bunny! He danced around in front of me and then waved before turning into several butterflies and flitting off in various directions. At that point I turned around, but it was just my dad standing there with a lamp. The last part of this 'silhouette show' was way out of his league... I would say impossible.... So, I cannot account for what I saw.

I actually revisit the subject of weird or false memories in the Arena album, 'Double Vision'.

Supplemental

This song has served me well over the years. It works so well for just acoustic guitar and voice. I have used it in various guises... it is a particular favourite of mine at house gigs. I do hear from the various guitarists who have played this song with me, that this song consists of a lot of chords, and many of them are 'very similar', which makes it particularly tricky to play. I'm not a guitarist, so I wouldn't know.

Mad as a Hatter

The third Shadowland album. This album was released in 1996, but, by now, we were all starting to get busy with other things, and sadly this meant inactivity for Shadowland. It was not long after bringing out 'Hatter' that the band went on hiatus until 2009.

U.S.I. (United States of Insanity)

Have faith, my friends
Listen to my story - this story never ends
You heard it here first, my son
We have got to be the only ones

Caught in possession of a Wednesday afternoon
Break point! Energy deserted us too soon
Desperate procession of partners caught in crime, crime, crime!
High frustration, down and drowning - sinking deep in time

Believe in me, follow and I'll talk you through
These anecdotes and mysteries
You heard it here first, my son
We have got to be the only ones

Trapped in the corner with a national holiday
Break point! Talking hard with nothing left to say

Thick smoke, whispered wreaths
Snaking through the heavy air
Fast food attitudes
Chemicals and angry stares

We just sit here making mountains out of molehills
Climbing up the ladder that can lead to nowhere fast!

Force feed new creeds
Tales of ghosts and severed hands
Hyperactive rollercoasters
Shooting through the mad Badlands

Strange news, changing views
Roll across the blood-stained floor
Spirit guides remain outside
Peering through the open doors

We just sit here making mountains out of molehills
Climbing up the ladder that can lead to nowhere fast!

Acid rain, bourbon stains
Soaking into open minds
ESP, law degrees, the inner souls of all mankind
UFOs, someone knows the truth is always out there!
Governments and cover-ups, the truth is always out there!

We just sit here making mountains out of molehills
Climbing up the ladder that can lead to nowhere fast!
We just sit here making mountains out of molehills
Climbing up the ladder that can lead to nowhere fast!

Look at these eyes, my child
I offer what's real - there are no such things as lies
Cling to these words, my child
Stay by my side - you must be nearly mine
Hold onto this hand, my child
This is your chance - there are no such things as lies

They are pawns in the game of power
Someone else's choosing
Just part of the jigsaw puzzle
Coloured with rhyme and reason

I am walking up a one way street
I can't go back, there's no repeat
I am holding to the burning rose
I sense no pain, I feel no heat

We sit here in united states, challenging fates and nations
Uttering words to calm the nerves of volatile relationships
We sit here in united states, planning these assassinations
Offer the thoughts that wise men taught of hope and dedication

We sit here in united states of insanity
"U.S.I... U.S.I... U.S.I... U.S.I..."

Behind the Lyric

*`Have you guessed the riddle yet?' the Hatter said, turning to Alice again.
`No, I give it up,' Alice replied: `what's the answer?'
`I haven't the slightest idea,' said the Hatter.*
                    Lewis Carroll, Alice's Adventures in Wonderland

Again, I was channelling the Lewis Carroll vibe for this one. I have described the lyrics of Shadowland as 'nightmares, nonsense and nursery rhymes' - this is a particularly good example.

I also use this song as a kind of Shadowland retrospective and I have referred back to some older themes: the rose, the jigsaw and the one-way street, for example.

Supplemental

This song featured one of my absolute favourite bits to sing, despite the large number of lyrics! The 'thick smoke, whispered wreaths' section had terrific energy and, strangely, I could remember the words, even though it was virtually a tongue twister.

This is the first album in which others contributed to the music. Mike Varty added material for this track.

Mephisto Bridge

Living all the fantasies - Heroes and heroic deeds
Hiding in the shadows - You don't know me
Living all the memories - Other people other places
There's a smile from the other side
From a man in a mask with far too much to hide

You can lean on me, my friend
You can trust me to defend you

Living at the edge of the world
A sight half seen, a sound half heard
Hiding in the shadows - You don't know me
You can choose one side of the other
The path you take will be the one for ever - Follow me, follow me

Beyond this line is an alien side - A place that exists in your mind
There is no light and there is no guide
A place that exists in your mind

Mephisto Bridge - this is the gateway
Opposite fates and intricate faces
Which one is mine? Which is my life? - Please show me!

This way is dark, and this way is light
But stand in the centre and both sides are right
This is place you will finally find
It's always been there in your mind

Mephisto Bridge - it lies in the middle
A way to salvation? A path to the devil?
Which is my side? Which is my life? - Please show me!
Mephisto Bridge - it crosses the chasm
There is the dream and there is the master
Which is my side? - Which is my life? - Please show me!

It's all wrong now - I don't know anymore
I don't care anymore
Why can't you show me?!
Makes no sense now - I can't see anymore
I can't feel anymore
Why can't you show me, show me, show me, show me?!

Behind the Lyric

This song has a special place in my heart. It comes from another of my weird dreams, where I found myself having to cross an extremely precarious bridge over some kind of bottomless ravine. The problem was that my dream began on the bridge and I was not sure which side I was trying to get to. I was aware that one side would eventually lead me to safety and the other would eventually lead me to some kind of hell, but they both looked thoroughly uninviting!

Supplemental

This dream left me with a strong image for quite some time, so it only seemed right to put a song together called 'The Devil's Bridge', or as I eventually called it, 'Mephisto Bridge'. I reached this title with a little help from Franz Liszt ('Mephisto Waltz').

For some reason the dilemma of this bridge has remained a strong influence in various things I have written, and I often use this heading as a working title for other things that I am developing. For example, I have written a novel (never published), which I called 'Mephisto Bridge', and the working title for the third 'Alchemy' musical is 'Mephisto Bridge', although I doubt that this will be the final title.

Flatline

Flatline - Look for a sign, run behind the afterlife
Today is a good day to die, waiting for a chance to reach the light
Flatline - Look for a sign, run behind the afterlife

Have you ever gone past that line? Cold and numb
Have you been to the other side? Fighting back the need to run
Did you ever think what came next?
Did you ever think what came next?
Have you ever seen death close up? Stare into your soul
Have you ever stood quite so near? It's tapping on you shoulder

Flatline - Look for a sign, run behind the afterlife
Today is a good day to die, waiting for a chance to reach the light
Flatline - Nowhere to hide, follow behind the afterlife
Today is a good day to die
Waiting for a chance to reach out to the light

Following the team game never to be seen again
There is always someone else to blame it on
When the promises and broken hopes have fallen down
There is always someone else to blame it on
Someone out there!

Flatline - Look for a sign, running behind the afterlife
Today is a good day to die, waiting for a chance to reach the light
Flatline - Nowhere to hide, follow behind the afterlife
Today is a good day to die
Waiting for a chance to reach out to the light
Flatline - Passing them by, taking up the risk to stay alive
Flatline - Passing them by
Taking up the risk that we may all survive

Behind the Lyric

'Today is a good day to die'.
                    Kiefer Sutherland in *Flatliners*

It is probably fairly obvious, but I had just watched the 1990 film *Flatliners* with Kiefer Sutherland and Julia Roberts. This is a movie full of interesting questions, as well as disturbing ideas and vivid images. It is also a story of redemption, which appeals to my nature, and is something I have employed in many concepts and stories I have written.

Supplemental

The music for this song was actually written by Mike Varty and Ian Salmon, so for me it was all about adjusting the structure to work with my lyrics and vocal lines. To be honest, I find it easier to write alone, but then again, many of the co-writes I have been a part of have yielded great results.

The Seventh Year

Part one: "A Curious Tale"

Staring across the water front
She can see Africa from here
"Oh Romeo, Romeo, wherefore art thou, Romeo...?"
There's no need to shed those tears

They wait for the light to touch them now
They wait for the world to pass them by
Hanging to each other as they spin into infinity
"Hush little baby, don't you cry"

Watch those ripples go racing from the centre point
How can this mere illusion fail?
"Oh Romeo, Romeo, where the hell are you, Romeo?
His life is such a curious tale"...

Part two: "Why Kruhulick?"

Behind the Lyric

Well, this is mainly an instrumental, so referring back to Mr. Kruhulick seemed like a nice idea.

I can remember one thing about the opening part, 'A Curious Tale'. I was sitting on a bench in the Isle of Dogs (London Docklands), looking over the water towards Canary Wharf – a business district containing some of the tallest buildings in London. If you stamp your metaphorical feet there, then ripples would flow out across the world. It takes a lot of money, lies and heartbreak to make a place like that. This is what inspired me to write the lyrics.

I needed a title for this rather random two-part track. Since I had decided that part two could be a reference back to the 'The Kruhulick Syndrome' with its title of 'Why Kruhulick', I thought that the overall title should perhaps be a related reference. Mr. Kruhulick, as I said earlier, was a character in *The Seven Year Itch* movie starring Marilyn Monroe. That led me to call the track 'The Seventh Year'. In truth there is no real connection with that and the lyrical subject matter of part one, which I simply called 'A Curious Tale'.

Supplemental

In all honesty I have no recollection of playing this track on stage, so, instead, I offer you...

Seven Useful Facts about Shadowland:

1. One venue had a poster outside announcing our gig in the name of 'ShadowLAD'... maybe we should have gone for the 'boy band' image.
2. The uniform of the band, certainly for the first few tours, were the long black coats, or 'duster coats'. I remember you could get these easily at Camden Market in London for about 20 pounds. You cannot anymore!
3. To 'add' to the performance of the song 'Jigsaw' I got a load of jigsaw pieces spray-painted black. I used to chuck them into the audience during the song. After the gigs I would always check the auditorium floor just to make sure people

were taking the pieces away with them.

4. During the last tour, if we needed to look on 'the bright side' at any point, we made use of a famous Mark Westwood quote... 'It's always Christmas somewhere in the world'.

5. A flight case that we nicknamed 'the coffin' was built for us during the early Shadowland tours. It was designed so we could carry a couple of keyboards in one box. I still use that old and battered case now, to carry my 360-degree rotating stand.

6. There is a folder on a stored hard disk that has some unused Shadowland material. It would take quite a bit of detective work to restore anything into a listenable format, but I can say that the working title of the fourth album was 'Charades'.

7. On the first Shadowland tour, we all set off eagerly on our way to our first gig, in Belgium. The organisation was not as good as it needed to be, however, because our navigator managed to take us to Winchester instead of Dover! Needless to say, we missed our ferry, and we arrived late. I like to think that things improved after that!

Father

What goes around comes around once again
You know we can't leave these things still and unchanged
When you're standing alone on the edge of the world
There is no going back so I've heard
Beyond this point is an alien side
A place that existed within my own mind
Searching the world we look for a sign
Waiting and crossing that line

Look at the man with the fear in his eyes
As he follows the blood of his fathers
Look at the girl with the tears in her eyes
As she wipes the blood from her face

Living the fantasies, heroes and deeds
Hide in the shadows, you'll never see me
When you enter the house with the treacherous mouse
You know that you'll never be free,
Putting the jigsaw together again
Still there are chasms and gaps that remain
When you're living a lie in an act of defiance
How can you ever be free?

Look at the man with the fear in his eyes
As he follows the blood of his fathers
Look at the girl with the tears in her eyes
As she follows the blood of her fathers

Let there be one who can hear me right now
As I fall to the ground in a negligent crowd
What goes around comes around once again
You know that you'll never be free!
Look at the man with the fear in his eyes
As he follows the blood of his fathers
Look at the girl with the tears in her eyes
As she follows the blood of her fathers

Behind the Lyric

For a while I had wanted to write a more folky song, but still with a dark twist. I had watched a film where a girl was 'guided' to do various things through the will of her dead father. Towards the end it becomes a battle of strength between them, although there is still no clearly defined good or evil side. The bond between them is both good and bad!

You may notice that in the 'living the fantasies' segment there is a reference to a 'treacherous mouse'. I am not sure I have publicly shared this before, but that was just a line I put in while I was writing the lyrics. It was supposed to be temporary until I could find the right thing to say. Sadly, the mouse grew on me, and in the end, I just left it there! If you happen to have the version of the album with the 'Pete Nichols' (singer from IQ) artwork, you will see that I got him to reinforce the mouse image in the CD booklet!

Supplemental

Between you and me… on the 'Mad as a Hatter' album I am not too happy with the end of this song… The tuning was not good enough, and every time I heard it I would find my teeth clenching.

I took the opportunity to re-record the song as a bonus track on a Caamora album ('Journey's End')… I can relax now!

The Burning

Tears of rage coursing down like molten lava
Angry cries ringing out like the first primal scream
Clenched fists held out in knotted and frustrated statement
Heavy frowns, pressing down into the pit
Why should I live with this? How can I live with this?

Sexual passion hide behind the thin veneer of politics
Jealousies waved around with the rope and the chain
Never understanding - fundamental reasoning
Devoid of all communication, barren of all thought persuasion

Burning, burning, raging like fire in a world of hate
Exiled and bleeding, misleading
Lost in a nightmare - a frightened state, out of control

Cynics and barbarians bringing nations to their knees
Cult fanatics selling values - reveries
New extremes of evolution spawning freaks and soul pollution
Cornered in exquisite chaos, letting go of something

Burning, burning, raging like
Fire in a world of hate
Exiled and bleeding, misleading
Lost in a nightmare - a frightened state
Beaten and kneeling, screaming
Tortured and sightless, a tireless fate
Forever burning, burning
Lust for revenge in a fragile place, out of control

Burning, burning, raging like fire in a world of hate
Exiled and bleeding, misleading
Lost in a nightmare - a frightened state
Beaten and kneeling, screaming
Tortured and sightless, a tireless fate
Forever burning, burning
Lust for revenge in a fragile place, out of control

Behind the Lyric

Despite the title, this was not inspired by the 1981 'slasher movie' of the same name. This was simply another of my 'feverish dream' tracks.

Supplemental

This is the other of the Shadowland tracks for which I did not write the music. Mike Varty did the music for this one.

Mad As A Hatter

Please don't try to see through these eyes
You couldn't live with what you'd find
Please don't try to think with this mind
You might be drawn into this nightmare

And don't believe that you can fool me
Your patient smile and boundless energy
My own peculiar brand of sanity
May take me from this room... too soon...

Men with heads and crazy faces chase me down the treacle aisle
Thunder bolts and undone laces leave me with no place to hide

Dodging swords and household creatures
Falling down those endless stairs
Empty friends with empty features
Offer no escape, they simply stare

All my life there's someone out there
Guiding me to climb so high that I may reach a new existence
Pray hard - feel good - and you - you should
Achieve your goal - they know!

All my life there's something out there
Guiding me to do what's right and I will be the one rewarded
Head down - heart strong - it won't be long
I'll be accepting all those gifts

Looking for pigs in the cemetery
All I can find are angels' wings
Fallen beliefs, long lost dreams and feelings - healings?
Feeding the bears with my old school cap
There goes my brother to get the cap back
Memories change, never the same and they're fading - degrading?
Playing with gods in the woods and the fields
How could this possibly fail to be real?

Holding your breath, seconds from death - and daring -
despairing?

So this is where I am, playing with shadows in a far darker land
When I play this flute, you'll follow me now, follow me now
And sing this tune, you'll follow me round and round and round
When I wave my hand, you'll follow me now, follow me now
Take my hand and follow me round and round and round

Fantasy is the final resting place for long lost hope

I don't want to see through your eyes
I couldn't live with what I'd find
I don't want to think with your mind
I might be drawn into this nightmare

Praying mantis on my shoulder, whispered bastard sentiments
Heavy feathers, flying boulders
Father, can't you see, I am lost beyond all hope and grace!

All my life there's someone out there
Guiding me to climb so high that I may reach a new existence
All my life there's something out there
Guiding me to do what's right and I will be the one rewarded
All my life there's someone out there
Calling me to change my life
And turn my back on ghosts and demons

Promises and secret kisses
They all just turn to stone or burn to ashes...

Behind the Lyric

Lewis Carroll, *Alice in Wonderland*

And we are, of course, back to Lewis Carroll again. For a couple of months I tried keeping a 'dream notebook'. This song was a result of all the strange and disjointed elements that floated through my head during this time. Do not ask me for meanings behind this lot – I would need to have a chat with my subconscious!

Supplemental

There was at some point a plan to reflect the Mad Hatter's tea party in the stage performance of this song. Initially, we were just talking about a few hats, but in no time the ideas grew into costumes and stage sets. It would have been quite a colourful affair, but sadly the realities of budget crept in, and we finally opted for 'nothing' instead. Somehow, me just putting on a hat did not seem quite enough!

I notice that I make a reference to another false memory I have:

'Feeding the bears with my old school cap
There goes my brother to get the cap back'

This is referring to a memory I have of going to the zoo with my parents. I was still wearing school uniform (we went to school on Saturday mornings, and I think we went straight onto the zoo from there). For some reason, while we were looking at some bears, I decided to throw them my cap. Well, I was only six, I think. My memory assures me what happened next was that my mum managed to get into the bear enclosure, scare back the bears, and retrieve the cap. This, of course, is not the case. I have it on good authority (my mum!) that the bears shredded the cap! In this song I credit 'my brother' with getting the cap back, although I do not have a brother.

I pick up the false memory theme again some years later in Arena. I must have forgotten making use of this zoo anecdote in the 'Mad as a Hatter' album, because there is another reference to the bears in the song 'Zhivago Wolf', which is the first song on the 'Double Vision' album:

Could it be I threw my cap into the ring?
Could it be she really tamed those bears?

Something else I noticed when I was checking the lyrics for this song: In the section with the lyric 'I don't want to see through your eyes', I have plundered some old material. This was originally an organ riff I wrote for a Sleepwalker song called 'Storms'. This Sleepwalker song also featured the nursery rhyme line, 'It's raining, it's pouring, the old man's snoring', which I again used back in the 'Ring of Roses' album, in the track, 'Scared of the Dark'.

In case anyone is wondering what is actually being said in that mysterious and dark backwards voice at the end of the song, I can tell you…

'Shadowland features Clive Nolan, Karl Groom, Mike Varty, Ian Salmon and Nick Harradence.'

Salvation Comes

Try to make those loose ends meet
Holding on - keep my feet on the ground
I need to have that sinner's heart
Shrouded hope - I'm sending this message to you
Is there one who can hear me now
Shouting "help" from a lonely room
Fallen down in a sightless crowd
Onto cold and unforgiving shards of stone

Reaching out your hand to my brow
I am crying for your healing touch
Never sure what's right or wrong
Knowing what I fell is just not enough

Your life and soul are a part of me
Fire and passion could be more than a dream
Reading signs into everything
Only you can know that I am waiting in darkness to see

Reaching out your hand to my brow
I am crying for your healing touch
Never sure what's right or wrong
Knowing what I feel is just not enough

More than this is not easy to say
Could it be that I am scared this time?
Letting go of all those promises
I always hide behind my own kind of safety net

Reaching out your hand to my brow
I am crying for your healing touch
Never sure what's right or wrong
Knowing what I fell is just not enough

Venom runs across the world unseen
Every day - the more we live the more we bleed

Only can the future lie beyond extremes
Knowing this I wonder where does my pathway lead?
Reaching out my heart to you
I dance in fire till salvation comes
A cry for help - a simple truth
And in the end I know that we are the lonely ones

Reaching out my heart to you
Reaching out my heart to you
Reaching out my heart to you
Reaching out my heart to you

Behind the Lyric

I wanted to write something that has a more choral sound - almost a gospel feel, perhaps. I found a great sound on a 'Korg Wavestation keyboard module', and that provided me with the foundation for the song. I also think it helped that I dragged a few guest voices into the mix... Martin Orford, Martin Ogden, Paul and Thérèse Wrightson, Damian Wilson, Mike Varty, Ian Salmon, Tracy Hitchings and Dave Wagstaffe.

Supplemental

The funny thing is that Shadowland never performed this song live, but it has been performed in more recent years. In the last ten years I have performed quite a few house gigs (little concerts, literally done in people's houses).

One of my favourite 'venues' is in France, where I have performed almost every year for quite some time now. This has been hosted by my good friends Agnes and Thomas Konsler. At two of these gigs, people have got together and performed this song for me. The first time, it was performed by some guest musicians, including some from a band called Weend'o. The second time was as a birthday surprise for me. The house gig was happening on my birthday, and also a ridiculously hot day (40 degrees)! I was taken on a trip to buy wine while, unbeknownst to me, some of my friends who were there, along with the guest musicians, rehearsed the song, which they performed for me at the end of the night. That was a lovely surprise!

Extras!

As a result of various re-releases, as well as an EP and the 'best of' album, there are a handful of songs that do not fit on the three main studio albums.

Edge of Night

Don't put your hand in the fire
Don't try and play where the water's too deep
Don't climb that wall
When Icarus tried to fly higher
Did he listen to warnings of what he would reap?
How far would he fall?

Better the truth than a lie
The warnings ignored and the prophetic cries
Lost second sight
When visions are clear as the first blinding light
Then your choice is to run or to dance
Dance on the edge of the night

What will you do on the edge of the night?
What will you do on the edge of the night?
You've gone too far
You played the role
You crossed the line
You sold your soul
What will you do on the edge of the night?

Don't ever stray from the path
Don't let the vampire enter your home
Don't be too proud
Never leave fear in your heart
Or the wolf inside may break out – free to hunt you down

Can you remember all the flavours?
Can you remember all the colours of your nightmares?
Can you remember all the flavours?
Can you remember all the shades of your nightmares?
Your nightmares!

What will you do on the edge of the night?
What will you do on the edge of the night?
You've gone too far
You played the role
You crossed the line
You sold your soul
What will you do on the edge of the night?

Can you remember all the flavours?
Can you remember all the colours of your nightmares?
Can you remember all the flavours?
Can you remember all the shades of your nightmares?

Don't put a new pair of shoes on the table
Don't let that umbrella open inside
Never deny all those cautionary tales
The moment may come when it's too late to hide
Severed heads and fortune-tellers
Is it for real when the fat lady sings?
Bell book and candle, the tools of the exorcist
These are a few of my favourite things

Pierrot dolls and old rocking chairs
Trees hit by lightning and lost severed limbs
Curses and verses and foreign affairs
Anthems of hatred and venomous hymns
Clowns that wait at the end of your bed
Pulling the sheets as you hide from your sins
Running in dreams with your shoes made of lead
These are a few of my favourite things

What will you do on the edge of the night?
What will you do on the edge of the night?
You've gone too far
You played the role
You crossed the line
You sold your soul
What will you do on the edge of the night?
What will you do on the edge of the night?
You've gone too far
You played the role
You crossed the line
You sold your soul
What will you do on the edge of the night?
What will you do on the edge of the night?

Behind the Lyric

I was actually in the middle of writing material for 'She' (the musical). I remember that I had been doing an interview earlier that day, and we had ended up discussing Shadowland in some detail. I guess that must have triggered some deep-seated nostalgia in me, because, while I was working on some new material ideas later in the day, I realised that I was writing a Shadowland song and not anything suitable for 'She'. Regardless, I carried on and created 'Edge of Night'.

The music came quickly, but the lyrics came even quicker, and it was obviously a return to my 'nightmare worlds', with plenty of superstition and old wives' tales thrown in... and it comes complete with a special nod towards musicals after all: namely *The Sound of Music* and the 'Favourite Things' reference.

Supplemental

Having written this song, it got me thinking about 'getting the band back together'! It seemed to be very much the right time to do this, and so I asked the other guys.

Karl Groom was ready and willing, as was Mike Varty and Nick Harradence. Ian was unavailable, hence we recruited Mark Westwood on bass guitar.

I also contacted Jadis who had been our partners in the legendary (in our minds) 'Lurv Ambassadors' tour, and suggested we went out together. With this in place, we all headed back out on tour in 2009.

I was not ready to write and record a whole new album, but we did bring out a 'best of', featuring a special recording of this new 'Edge of Night' track, and we also filmed the show in Poland which lead to the 'Edge of Night' DVD and the 'Cautionary Tales' box set.

Dorian Gray

The dust across this picture
Shows negligence of age
Just emptiness and solitude
To wipe the tears away
There's sadness in the eyes
As they're staring back at me - So painfully

I don't regret a word I said
Don't forget a word I said - I know!

There's a guilt upon the canvas
I see hatred in the frame
It's a multi - coloured testament
To wipe the tears away
Distorted mirror images
No second chance to say "please forgive me"

I can't hide from you
I can't hide from you!

But should I wait or run from here
Or stand and face my Dorian Gray?
With passing days and passing years
Too dangerous a game for me to play?

I've got a sentimental fever
Warning me of any changes made
I've got to paint the non - believer out
Avoid the path he lays
He's reaching out to touch me now
Before the judgment time
I've got to change the picture on the wall
It's mine! It's mine!

I don't regret a word I said
Don't forget a word I said
Picture on the wall - "You know!"

Behind the Lyric

The 'corruption of eternal life' has been a constant subject of interest for me since childhood. I remember being particularly disturbed when I saw the old Hammer film version of *She* – it gave me nightmares for weeks, but it also fascinated me: the idea of eternal life and the inevitable dark consequences of such a quest or craving.

This 'idée fixe' has crept out in various guises throughout my work – most obviously with 'She' the musical, but also with 'Half Moon Street', parts of 'Jigsaw' and, of course, this song inspired by the Oscar Wilde story.

Supplemental

True fact: I do have a portrait of myself sitting in the attic. I have not looked at it since it was put up there, some years ago.

Who knows... maybe it helps!

I, Judas

I, Judas! Standing in the crowd
High on empty gestures
Wearing friendship like a shroud
With a morbid sense of purpose, I'm waiting for the day
When your back is turned
When you're too far away!

I, Judas! Will support you to the hilt
Like the knife that rests between your ribs
A symbol of my faith and of my guilt...
You can strike with the poison of a serpent in the grass
With protection as a feature
Of your altruistic mask

So Judas! Is it all as it appears
With your heart on your sleeve
With your crocodile tears!
The victims crying "Traitor! Traitor!"
Your freedom's gone!
Do you wish to spend that silver now?
Same story - new song?

Judas! Is your reputation safe?
Will you blame it on circumstances
Will you blame it on the impudence of fate?
You can pull till the crooked world blows itself apart
With corruption flowing strongly
Round your philanthropic heart

When you look down the barrel of a firing squad
You can turn to stone
You can pray to your God
Stand fast! Stand firm!
There's a way to break the chains
I do not feel for anyone - I do not kneel to anyone
Now I know your name!

So Judas!
When you're walking through your dreams
There's a tear in the fabric of the world you built
It's coming apart at the seams
Judas!
Keep an eye in the back of your head
'Cause I'm still here
Not down! Not out! Not dead!

Keep an eye in the back of your head
Keep an eye in the back of your head
'Cause I'm still here
Not down! Not out! Not dead!

Behind the Lyric

I wanted to write an angry song: something that spat venom. A song of betrayal, treachery and revenge. Well, here it is!

I was interested in exploring a slightly heavier rock sound, and it occurs to me that perhaps this was the beginning of my shift across to Arena.

Supplemental

I have mentioned the problems with remembering lyrics a few times through this book. Let me do it one more time…

We were performing this song – I believe it was at a Classic Rock Society gig up in Rotherham, UK. As we launched into the music, something in the audience caught my eye. I really cannot recall what that was, but it threw my concentration for a moment, and I realised I could not remember any of these lyrics, apart from the last few lines… 'keep an eye in the back of your head'.

This was a textbook case of 'singing in Chinese' as I stumbled my way through this song, singing complete and utter nonsense. Every now and then I found a few correct words along the way and enjoyed great relief once we got to the end bit, which I did remember.

The funny thing was, that after the gig, I apologised to the band for the mess up, and none of them had even noticed…

Hardly worth learning all these lyrics in the first place!

Phantoms

For those in peril in their lives
Never heed the phantom's call
This song will draw your spirit in
And leave you wrecked upon the shore

Steer your ship to safer waters
Far beyond beguiling sounds
Steer your ship to safer waters
And one day you shall return to land

Shut your mind to all temptation
Beauty here is merely false
Turn away from this illusion
The evil power that this place holds

For those in peril in their lives
Never heed the phantom's call
This song will draw your spirit in
And leave you wrecked upon the shore

Behind the Lyric and Supplemental

This song really was a bit of an afterthought. I was told very late on that we had to provide a bonus track for the Japanese release of 'Hatter'. I had to produce something that day, and the band were not around. Two ideas then converged to make this little ditty.

I had just been watching a bit of *The Sound of Music* on TV, when I heard I needed this extra track. Having just been listening to 'Climb Every Mountain' I decided to write something with a tongue in cheek nod in that direction… this explains the 'extra cheese' level on this one.

I had also been considering various concepts for Arena, and the 'Siren' analogy was at the front of my mind, so I made use of that. Naturally, this came to a greater and more solid fruition on Arena's 'Pride' album with the track 'Sirens'.

So, the Music Stops

Don't lie to me - Now more than ever
Don't live with this alone
Were you ever going to share with anyone

I stand alone, and I remember
The last thing you said to the world
Was "So the music stops"

Is there fear in that heart of yours
Do you believe the promises they made
And are there doubts, or second thoughts
As you march towards the light
With your eyes still open...

Oh, have faith in the people you know
They won't let you down

And is there fear in that heart of yours
Do you believe the promises they made
And are there doubts or second thoughts
As you march towards the light
With your eyes still open...

Don't turn away from me forever
I found myself believing
There could be something more than this

Don't hide yourself away forever
And the last thing you said to the world
Was so the music stops

And the last thing you said to the world
Was so the music stops

Behind the Lyric and Supplemental

This was a hard song to write. My Casino writing partner in crime, Geoff Mann had died of cancer. This had been a terrible shock for all those around him, as well as all the Twelfth Night fans out there.

Geoff and I had been planning to make a sequel album to Casino, but his health had robbed us of that opportunity. I had even started some musical ideas, and the album was going to be called 'My Brother's Keeper' based around the Cain and Abel biblical story.

I was told, shortly after his death, that the last words he spoke were, 'So, the music stops'.

And there you have it!

The Shadowland lyrics collected together in one place. I hope you have enjoyed some of my ramblings, and maybe it will encourage you to dig out those albums and DVDs again... or if you don't know the band, here is your chance!

Just one more thing before I finish. I really must mention one of our staunchest supporters, and my friend, Patric Toms: known to his closest friends as 'Magus'. Sadly, he passed away in April 2020, but we have a history of adventures together. Something I will always remember is that he came out as the tour manager for the 'Lurv Ambassadors' tour, which I have mentioned earlier. This tour was a two-band extravaganza with Shadowland and Jadis. In east Germany Patric managed to procure a Russian hat and a telescope, which he then clung to for the remainder of the tour. He was always looking for reasons to wear the hat… and to use the telescope.
He found them!

ABOUT THE AUTHOR

Clive Nolan is a British musician, composer and producer who has played a prominent role in the recent development of progressive and symphonic rock. Born in Gloucestershire, he was a pupil at Wycliffe College and King's School, Gloucester. He completed his B. Mus and M. Mus degrees at London University where he studied composition, orchestration and conducting. He has been the regular keyboard player in Pendragon (1986–present), Shadowland (1992–present), Strangers on a Train (1993–1994), Arena (1995–present) and Caamora (2006–present) as well as writing music and lyrics for Arena, Shadowland, Caamora and numerous other projects.

Nolan is the founder member of the Caamora Theatre Company, formed to produce and perform his musicals. The premiere of the rock opera 'She' took place at the Wyspiański Theatre in Katowice, Poland in October 2007. Subsequently, full theatrical shows of 'She' were performed in January 2010 in Santa Cruz, Bolivia, followed by concert and theatre productions staged in the Netherlands, UK and Germany between 2011 and 2016.

Clive's second musical 'Alchemy', with libretto based on his original story, was released on CD in 2013. Soon after, the live show was recorded for DVD in Poland. Between 2013 and 2017, 'Alchemy' toured the European stages, including the London Off-West End Jermyn Street Theatre in 2014.

In 2016 the Norwegian branch of Caamora was formed from the initiative of the founder member of the 'Hurum Progrock Society', Morten L. Clason. Caamora Norway 'Alchemy' shows featuring Clive and the otherwise all-Norwegian cast were performed in Norway in 2017. The show at the historical Høytorp Fort in Mysen was released on DVD in 2018.

In October 2016, Clive performed a series of concerts in Uruguay and Norway accompanied by acclaimed opera and musical theatre artists.

Clive's third musical 'King's Ransom' was released on CD and premiered on stage at the Cheltenham Playhouse in September 2017. The show returned to the stage a year later in memory of the Caamora Theatre Company's late director, Ian Baldwin.

In 2018 Clive signed both 'Alchemy' and 'King's Ransom' to a film company with a view to bringing these musicals to the silver screen under the title 'The Professor King Chronicles'.

Despite his relentless engagement in musicals, Clive has not been neglecting Arena, the rock band founded in 1995 together with the drummer Mick Pointer. A new album entitled 'The Theory of Molecular Inheritance' is due for release in 2020. It will be the tenth studio album in the band's history. The release will be followed by a European tour.

Clive's 2020 project 'Song of the Wildlands' is an ambitious concept album – a secular oratorio with libretto based on the oldest English poem, 'Beowulf'. The project will feature an orchestra, four soloists and a one-hundred-voice choir singing in Anglo-Saxon. The forthcoming album has been signed to the 'Crime Records' label in Norway.

The first quarter of 2020 kept Clive occupied with rehearsals for Pendragon's mammoth world tour promoting their new album 'Love over Fear'. Alas, less than halfway through, the tour got cancelled due to the increasing threat of the coronavirus spreading all over the continents.

During the pandemic lockdown, Clive released a series of original comedy songs, which were presented and warmly received on Facebook, YouTube and Instagram.

In summer 2020, Clive joined the team of Eric Bouillette's new project Imaginærium, where he was offered the role of the main composer and lyricist, as well as being asked to play keyboards and sing one of the solo parts. The release of the first album, 'The Rise of Medici' is scheduled for 2021.

AWARDS:

Clive was voted Best Keyboard Player by the Classic Rock Society eleven times between 1995 and 2019.

In 2010 the Bolivian government awarded him with the title of Honorary Visitor to Santa Cruz, Bolivia for his theatre work in the city of Santa Cruz.

In 2013 he was awarded the Polish MLWZ 'Golden Lexicon Award' for Outstanding Achievements in Music for his musical 'Alchemy'.

In 2019 he received a Gold Disc for his involvement in the Dragon Force album 'Inhuman Rampage'.

Shadowland on Stage:

Clive Nolan – Vocals and Piano

Karl Groom - Guitars

Nick Harradence - Drums

Mark Westwood – Bass and Acoustic Guitar

Mike Varty – Keyboards

Former Live Members:

Richard West – Keyboards

Ian Salmon – Bass and Acoustic Guitar

Discography:

Ring of Roses (1992)

(Reissued with two bonus tracks - 1997)

(Re-mastered with bonus tracks - 2009)

Through the Looking Glass (1994)

(Re-issued with one extra track – 1997)

(Re-mastered with bonus tracks - 2009)

Mad as a Hatter (1996)

A Matter of Perspective - Best of Shadowland (2009)

EP:

Dreams of the Ferryman (1994)

DVD:

Edge of Night (2009)

Box Set: Cautionary Tales (2009)

Credits:

All Lyrics and Narrative: Clive Nolan

Biography, Proofreading and Editing: Magdalena Grabias

Additional Proofreading: Sian Roberts

Front Cover Photography: Neil Palfreyman

Back Cover Photography: Bert Treep

Cover Formatting: Julia Stüber

Photographs and Artwork Inside the Book:

Page 10	Unknown
Page 11	Willem Klopper
Page 12	Album cover photo by Steven van der Hoeff
Page 20	Christine Piontek
Page 26	Marta Tłuszcz
Page 31	Willem Klopper
Page 35	Unknown
Page 36	Album cover concept and photo by Laura Chambers and Steven van der Hoeff
Page 37	Laura Chambers
Page 40	Unknown
Page 48	Bo Hansen
Page 51	Laura Chambers
Page 55	Michelle Young
Page 63	Lice cartoon by Ross Andrews
Page 67	Album cover picture by Peter Nicholls
Page 71	Part of the Shadowland DVD artwork
Page 81	Mouse cartoon by Peter Nicholls
Page 83	Neil Palfreyman
Page 91	DVD boxset cover artwork Ag
Page 102	Bert Treep
Page 103	Martin Ogden
Page 106	Malc Bernhard

www.clivenolan.net

shop.caamora.net

ISBN: 9798683068851

Printed in Great Britain
by Amazon

62343448R00061